*L'Amour
de Cassatt*
Cassatt's Love

Family
in French and English

Odéon Livre
Chicago
2019

by Ethan Safron

French Books
Chicago, LLC

ISBN-13:
978-1-947961-69-2

A read-aloud version of this title is available online. To access this video, you may scan the QR code below or type `ouilovebooks.com/cassatt-audio` into your web browser.

ouilovebooks.com/cassatt-audio

Mary

Meet Mary.

Mary is an American painter.

Mary lives in France.

Voici Mary.

Mary est une peintre américaine.

Mary habite en France.

Maman

Meet Katherine.

Katherine is Mary's **mother**.

Mary is Katherine's **daughter**.

Voici Katherine.

Katherine est **la mère** de Mary.

Mary est **la fille** de Katherine.

Papa

Meet Robert.

Robert is Katherine's husband.

Mary is Robert's **daughter**.

Voici Robert.

Robert est le mari de **Katherine**.

Mary est la fille de **Robert**.

Lydia

Meet Lydia.

Lydia is Mary's older sister.

Mary is Lydia's younger sister.

Voici Lydia.

Lydia est la sœur aînée de Mary.

Mary est la sœur cadette de Lydia.

Alexander

Meet Alexander.

Alexander is Mary's older brother.

Alexander is Lydia's younger brother.

Voici Alexander.

Alexander est le frère aîné de Mary.

Alexander est le frère cadet de Lydia.

Robert

Meet Robert.

Robert is Alexander's son.

Mary is Robert's aunt.

Voici Robert.

Robert est le fils d'Alexander.

Mary est la tante de Robert.

Ellen et Gard

Meet Gardner Jr. and Ellen Mary.

Gardner Jr. is Mary's nephew.

Ellen Mary is Mary's niece.

Voici Gardner Jr. et Ellen Mary.

Gardner Jr. est le neveu de Mary.

Ellen Mary est la nièce de Mary.

Ellen

Ellen is Mary's parents' granddaughter.
Mary's parents are her grandparents.

Ellen est la petite fille des parents de Mary.
Les parents de Mary sont ses grands-parents.

Gard Jr.

Lidya and Mary are Gard Jr.'s
aunts.
Robert is his cousin.

Lydia et Mary sont les tantes de
Gard Jr.
Robert est son cousin.

Meet some of Mary's friends.

Mary's friends are artists, too.

They make her happy.

Voici quelques amis de Mary.

Les amis de Mary sont artistes aussi.

Ils la rendent heureuse.

What is your family like?

Elle est comment, votre famille ?

Ma famille

My Family

Immediate family / La famille proche

English	Français
father	le père
mother	la mère
parents	les parents
brother	le frère
sister	la sœur
son	le fils
daughter	la fille
husband	le mari
wife	la femme

Extended family / La famille élargie

English	Français
grandfather	le grand-père
grandmother	la grand-mère
grandson	le petit-fils
granddaughter	la petite-fille
aunt	la tante
uncle	l'oncle
nephew	le neveu
niece	la nièce
cousin (m)	le cousin
cousin (f)	la cousine
friend (m)	l'ami
friend (f)	l'amie

Les tableaux / Paintings

On a Balcony, 1879. The Art Institute of Chicago. Oil on canvas.

Mary Cassatt Self-Portrait, 1880. National Portrait Gallery. Gouache on paper.

Lilacs in a Window, 1880. Private Collection. Oil on canvas.

Lydia Crocheting in the Garden at Marly, 1880. The Metropolitan Museum of Art. Oil on canvas.

A Woman and a Girl Driving, 1881. Philadelphia Museum of Art. Oil on canvas.

Master Robert Kelso Cassatt, 1882. Private Collection. Oil on canvas.

Portrait of Alexander J. Cassatt and His Son, Robert Kelso Cassatt, 1884. Philadelphia Museum of Art. Oil on canvas.

Mr. Robert S. Cassatt on Horseback, 1885. Private Collection. .

Mother and Child, 1889. Cincinnati Art Museum. Oil on canvas.

Mrs. Robert S. Cassatt, the Artist's Mother, 1889. de Young Museum. Oil on canvas.

Gardner and Ellen Mary Cassatt, 1899. The Metropolitan Museum of Art. Pastel on paper.

Ellen Mary Cassatt In A White Coat, c. 1896. Private Collection. Oil on canvas.

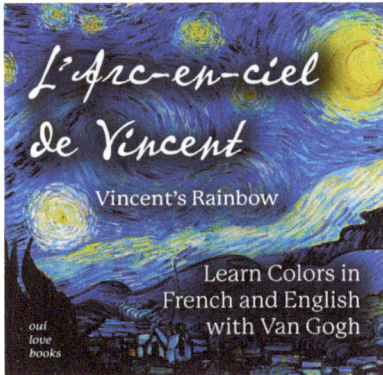

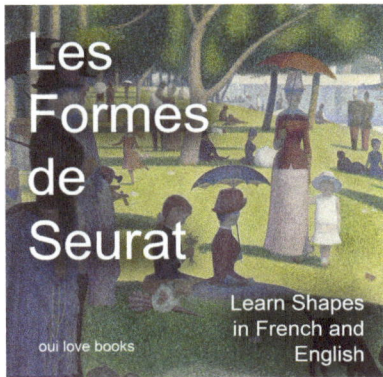

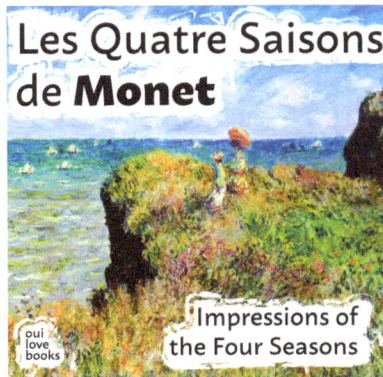

L'Arc-en-ciel de Vincent
Vincent's Rainbow
Learn Colors in French and English with Van Gogh

oui love books

Les Formes de Seurat
Learn Shapes in French and English

oui love books

Les Quatre Saisons de **Monet**
Impressions of the Four Seasons

oui love books

Le Paris de Caillebotte
City Life in French and English

oui love books

L'Amour de Cassatt
Cassatt's Love
Family in French and English

The

First Impressions

Series

FIN

www.ingramcontent.com/pod-product-compliance
Lightning Source LLC
LaVergne TN
LVHW072135070426
835513LV00003B/110